Finding Your Way

Alphabetical Keys to the Divine

Written By

Anita Kopacz

Written by Anita Kopacz
Foreword by Russell Simmons
Type Illustrations by Marisha Scott
Produced and Distributed by Augustus Publishing
Creative Direction & Design by Jason Claiborne

UPTOWN BOOKS July 2010
an imprint of Augustus Publishing

UPTOWN BOOKS | 113 East 125th Street NY, NY, 10035
www.uptownlife.net

UPTOWN BOOKS

Discover, Enrich & Inspire

FOREWORD

BY RUSSELL SIMMONS

In a world of complication and contrivance, it is refreshing to encounter the truth, plain and simple. This is how I felt when I was introduced to *Finding Your Way*. Anita walked toward me wearing all white, not unusual considering we were at Sean "Diddy" Combs' Annual White Party. What actually stood out was a glow of clarity and purpose, qualities which I recognize and respect. Anita asked me if she could randomly pick a page from the book, a practice she exercises each morning to maximize the day's potential for illumination and growth. She asked the universe for my message and opened the book to reveal W for Wisdom. As she read, I heard it; the Truth. I was particularly struck by the line, "Wisdom cannot be taught, it can only be remembered." I was intrigued, and when I later read the book in its entirety, I thought, 'This book is scripture, written for today.' The illustrations are compelling; jewel-like, they perfectly accentuate the gems of truth within. Simply put, *Finding Your Way* is a treasure, through and through. If you have read my book *Do You*, you know that I am moved by an individual's truth and how that truth is expressed. When asked to write this foreword, I was honored to help, not only Anita, but the Truth itself.

Art is the signature of one's soul. It is your individual gift from God.
Through art you are able to express your deepest feelings.

Fear has deemed it nearly impossible for many to find their true art form.
Release all forms of fear manifest and claim your artistic kingdom now!

We are children of the Most High and possess the divine capacity to create.
Art forges the ability in the artist to communicate on the level of the individual observer.
Art begets inspiration as inspiration begets art.

ART

May the channels of your artistic potential be cleared,
and your ability to create flow forth.

Being is the state bereft of trying.
It is your soul stripped down to the core no longer dependant on the labels pinned
upon you throughout existence. Being is freedom...
the entrance to the divine... the prerequisite of inner peace.
It is neither past nor future, it is the now. Being in the present is divine.
Be.
Be joyous.
Be sad.
Be yourself.
Be at peace and know that you are God.

For God is truth, and to be is the most honest form you can embody.

BEING

May your being rest upon the bosom of inner peace
and reflect the glory of God.

Courage is honesty wrapped in action.
It is your divine instinct before reason penetrates a situation.

The rose that grows through concrete knows naught of her limitations.
Her innate courage enables her miraculous feat.

Let not your courage be tainted by ego,
for true courage is a personal trophy shared with the divine.

Courage is recognizing fear and proceeding through it.
It is the knowledge of one's fate and ability.
Courage is fetched from the divine waters deep within your soul.

COURAGE

May courage bless your days with countless rewards.

Dance my children and be free.
Be free to experience the divine rhythm that sustains universal life.

The drums are her heartbeat and the flutes her breath.
Each step a jubilee and every twist a party.

Join in the celebration of life and feel the healing power of dance.

DANCE
May you release your inhibitions and dance.

Existence is the blank slate upon which we draw our individual realities.
There is no absolute existence but that of the Divine.

Our lives are dictated by our belief in existence.

For who believes in lack shall exist in lack,
and who believes in abundance shall exist in abundance.

We have been given the gift of molding our realities based upon our existence.

May we use this power to uplift ourselves,
and in doing so, enrich the lives of those around us.

EXISTENCE

Your existence is that of God.
May you mirror this gift in your reality.

Faith is doubtless. It is direct intention built upon the divine.

With faith, true faith, anything is possible.

The seed of doubt planted in the soil of intention shall soon become full grown.
Thus, faith-filled intention guarantees the surest deliverance of your goals
without the untimely manifestations of doubt.

Faith is the riverboat that safely carries you over the waters of fear.

FAITH

May your days reflect the faith of yesteryear
and may your future be bright with possibilities.

God is love. God is divine.
God is the beginning and the end; the alpha and the omega.
God is the professor of our lessons and comforter of our pains.
God is the ultimate creator and is everything created.

To place a label upon the Most High is a disservice to the universal quest of the divine.

God cannot be placed within a box, or within a paragraph for that matter.

The confinements meant to better understand the creator are not only in themselves elements of God, but representations of a false pretence established to separate good from evil.

Every polarity exists within the divine.
Everything is of God.

GOD

May you recognize your truth and see yourself in God.

Healing is the process of remembering the divine.

For in the return to God, all is remedied.

We are in a constant cycle of pain and healing.
Healing energy is contagious and can be transferred to those around us.

The same is true of pain.

Pain is merely an alarm to advise us of our diverted path.
Healing aids us in our return.

HEALING

May you recognize your faults without hesitation and begin your healing return to the divine.

Imagination represents the rudimentary understanding of your spirituality
and its level of maturity in the universe.

Limitless possibilities exist within your divine imagination.

Fear, nonetheless, possesses the ability to shape confinements
and limitations within this realm.

The seeds of manifestation are sown in your own imagination.
It cradles both the hopes and fears of the future.

Your capacity to imagine seems to dwindle as skepticism and doubt
encroach on its kingdom. Imagine. Imagine yourself free.
Free from fear and Free to simply Be.

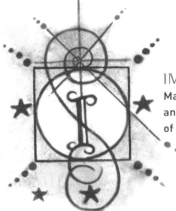

IMAGINATION

May your imagination be cured of disease and your true nature glorified in every stage of manifestation.

Joy is an emotion rooted in the divine. It cannot be swayed by the dramas of worldly origin.

Joy is a deep sense of divine happiness. It cannot be lost or stolen, for joy is a gift from God and is constantly available.

The art of remembering your joy and its rightful place within your space can often be clouded by fear... but your joy is always there.

JOY

May you look into the eyes of a child and
remember the joy that exists within us all.

Kindness is an art form of the divine.

As with many forms of art, either you are born with talent or you develop it over the years.

The universe thrives on divine kindness. For as you exhibit kindness to
others you elevate the vibrations of the entire universe.

Kindness encourages like action and creates a chain of events that stem from a single
act.
This mode of communication is a pipeline from the divine.

The ancestor of kindness is God, thus as we exhibit this
behavior so shall we be in line with the divine.

KINDNESS

May kindness ride the wings of your spirit and deliver you to the heaven that exists inside of you.

Love is an act of divine courage.

It can cradle one in sweet ecstasy or deliver a wound with piercing accuracy.

In love there are no rewards but the act itself.
Fear not love, yet never assume comradery. For love is neither friend nor foe.

If you embrace it, your life shall be full...full of joy and full of sorrow.
But if you run from it, your life shall be empty...you shall be empty.

Love.Love abundantly.
Love unconditionally.
Love.

LOVE

May the beauty of divine love color your spirit
and may the pain let you forget not your blessings.

A **miracle** portends any moment or act in which faith in God is restored.

Miracles linger in the ether poised and ready for their divine call.

There is no shortage of miracles, for they exist in every moment.

The perception altered towards the divine
shall experience the constant miracle that is God.

MIRACLES

May your everyday miracles be acknowledged
and may divine inspiration fill your heart.

Divine **nobility** exudes from the humble heart.

For when one learns from each lesson and assumes no arrogance,
true nobility is attained.

Ego is the wanting...not the knowing of one's greatness.

A true nobleman questions not his importance,
yet is humble in the eyes of God.

Nobility is the divine buoyancy factor that raises
insecurity to greatness and ego to humility.

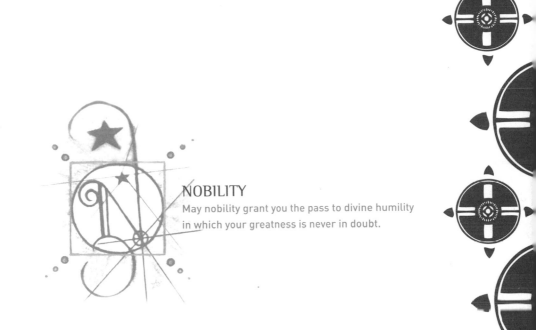

NOBILITY

May nobility grant you the pass to divine humility
in which your greatness is never in doubt.

Children are born with divine **openness** connected directly to the most high.

As our first days develop into years, doors close and
wide open innocence is replaced with skepticism and fear.

We must be open to receive our blessings.
We must allow the flow of the universe passage through our souls.

Open your eyes and see the divine.
Open your heart and feel the love.
Open your soul and find your purpose.

Be open and inspiration will find you.

OPENNESS

May divine openness rid your soul of doubt
and may your true purpose be revealed.

Passion is a fire that must be fed.

If ignored it can dissipate into a seemingly insignificant spark.

Passion is amplified truth.
It fears not judgment and seeks not approval.

Passion is concentrated intent executed with extreme emotion.
It allows for the deliverance of your art into the realm of the divine.

PASSION

May the passion within you be the guiding light
to the wealth within your soul.

Be **quiet** and find the beating of your heart.
Be still and remember your divine mother.

Lay and replenish. Restore the energy that you exude.

Forget not that the answers reside in the quiet air.
Only the wise take the time to listen.

Quiet yourself... Quiet your heart... Quiet your emotions... Quiet your soul.
Be still as you once were in your Earthly mother.

Receive the energy of divine sustenance through the universal umbilical cord.
Rest... for action is most appreciated after the calm.

QUIET
May you find peace in stillness and quiet the restless reverberance of your fears.

There exists a divine **rhythm** in everything...
a layer within us all that strives to be on beat.

We are aware of our follies and our missteps
that lead us to dance to the rhythm of life tone deaf to the divine.

Yet we pretend that our stumbles are choreographed numbers
and fail to learn our lessons.

Let us remember that rhythm is in line and freedom lies within the beat.
As we walk to the rhythm,

So shall we see... so shall we hear... so shall we speak... so shall we be.

RHYTHM

May divine rhythm lead your steps
to dance with the Most High.

The divine kingdom belongs to no one but is **shared** by all.
As we share our abundance so shall we receive.

The channel of giving and receiving are of the same source.
If you obstruct one of the two, the other will suffer as well.

Share the wealth of your soul with all. Let the world know your divinity.

Judge not who is worthy of your time, for every moment stems from the divine.
Share your heart... Share your ideas... Share your revelations without fear.

There is a wealth of abundance waiting to come forth in every aspect of your life.
Trust in the abundance and join the divine act of sharing.

SHARING
May your life overflow with blessings
as you find the courage to share.

Being **thankful** is the staple of the divine soul.
For as we appreciate our blessings, so shall they spring forth in abundance.

Every moment is deserving of thanks whether it is positive or negative.

For all is from God... the blessings and the lessons.

Give thanks and know that you are a deserving channel of the divine.
Give thanks and feel the joy of being humble.
Give thanks for your blessings.
Give thanks for your soul.

Humble yourself and feel the many gifts as they flow forth.

THANKSGIVING

May you recognize the divinity in every moment
and remain in a constant state of gratitude.

There is an underlying force that connects everything as the **universal** one.

We are intricate parts of a whole.
Each of us our own letter in the universal alphabet.
As we meet and share our divine knowledge, so are we able to better
understand the universal language.

For every letter we learn we whirl closer to our universality.

On our quest to the divine we are faced with many tests formatted to question our faith,
Yet, a mere change of perception alters those tests into proof of God.

For if we view the universal connection in everything,
the fact that these tests exist prove the existence of the divine.

UNIVERSAL

May you merge your soul into the universal one and flow gracefully with the divine.

The divine **void** is the birthplace of existence.

Before manifestation in the physical realm,
gestation in the realm of darkness is necessary.

The void is the womb of the divine.
Forever fruitful and constantly impregnated with seeds of intent.

Express divine caution while asking the void to create your desires,
For through this void anything is possible... positive or negative.

The divine void nurtures and presents a growing entity to all who ask.

VOID

May you possess grace and wisdom
in your interactions with the divine void.

Wisdom is the great wealth of divine knowledge
that stems from intuition.

Universal wisdom resides within us all.
It cannot be taught nor forgotten... It cannot be traded nor stolen.

Wisdom can only be remembered.
Remembered by the soul who wishes to be in line with God.

It is a way of life that emits peacefulness and grace.
It can only be retrieved from the well of the divine with complete faith.
This knowledge is bereft of doubt.

It offers guidance without question... It offers purposeful intent...
It offers ancient secrets discovered by our ancestors, if only we choose to remember.

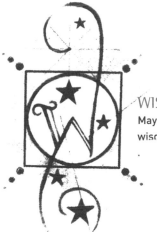

WISDOM

May you look inside yourself and remember that
wisdom is the sole knowledge of the divine.

The **X factor** represents the unknown...
the divine challenger and sustainer of faith.

Once we are able to accept the unknown within ourselves and our reality,
fear will dissipate and learning will commence.

As in mathematics, the divine X factor allots a space for the unknown...
a space for God.

The faith required to assign a name which acknowledges rather
than denies the existence of the unknown,

Allows one to build equations which yield actual information
about the universe and our position within it.

X FACTOR

May the X factor balance the equation of your life, and may your answers be the product of your search for the divine.

Yes I am worthy. Yes I am alive. Yes I am divine.

There are only two definitive answers to a request, YES and NO.

Yes is full of energy. Within it lays a seed ready to be
planted in the fertile ground of the request.

No kills the energy of the particular request and makes
room for new intentions to emerge.

Therefore the lesson is to choose. Do not linger in indecision.
For when your intentions are clear, YES grows into results and
NO creates a clearing for a new YES!

YES

May you shout out your intentions to the divine and when offered your gifts proudly proclaim, "Yes!"

Zenith is the highest point on the celestial sphere...
the actualization of your soul's divine aspirations.

It is the point of culmination...
the residence of your highest self.

As you look towards your zenith, your reflection burns bright with divinity.

Although your zenith may seem as unattainable as a mirage,
fear not; for the journey is the point itself.

As you strive to meet your zenith ,
it simultaneously rushes forth to meet you

ZENITH

May the journey to your zenith be swift and graceful,
culminating in an epiphanic explosion of each of these
alphabetical keys to the divine.